Workbook

For

Think Like A Monk

Train Your Mind For Peace and Purpose Everyday

Robin Reads

Table of Contents

About The Book

"Think Like a Monk: Train Your Mind for Peace and Purpose Every Day" is a self-help and motivation book. The author weaves his personal experiences as well as the wisdom and traditions of monks to teach us how to live less anxious and more purposeful lives. Jay Shetty shows us how these ancient teachings can still be applied to modern life. The book shares ideas and practices that monks live by and incorporates practical exercises.

In the introduction to the book, Jay differentiates between two mindsets: "Monk Mind" and "Monkey Mind". The monkey mind is a mind that overthinks, is easily distracted, prefers to multi-task, procrastinates, is self-centered and controlled by fear, worry, and anger. By contrast, the monk mind is calmer, more compassionate and collaborative, single-tasked, more focused, and patient.

This book shows you how to be a more mindful person and to make the switch from monkey mind to having a monk mind. It provides you with ways to help you connect with your inner being and live a fulfilling and meaningful life. In the book, Jay reveals how we can overcome negative thoughts and habits, fears, and anxieties to find happiness and peace of mind.

The book is broadly divided into three parts: let go (identity, negativity, fear, intention), grow (purpose, routine, the mind, ego), give (gratitude, relationships, service). Each part teaches specific lessons to enable us to practically apply the monks' way of thinking to our own busy lives. The teachings are interwoven with interesting anecdotes, stories, and practical examples. Shetty also shares some research that shows how some monk wisdoms are supported by science.

We learn how to identify who we are, how to find our true purpose, how to forgive, how to put aside ego, and how to serve others. We even learn how to breathe because Jay learned on his first day at the monastery that this is the first thing monks learn. Your breath is the only thing that stays with you throughout your life that does not change.

The book aims to help us learn how to live a more peaceful and contented life. The lessons are meant to inspire and empower us and to help us grow personally and spiritually.

About The Workbook

This workbook aims to help you take the ideas proposed in Think Like a Monk and apply them to your life in a practical way. The purpose of this workbook is to guide you in finding your way to a more meaningful life using the wisdoms from the book. The workbook takes you through a series of exercises designed to make you reflect and reconnect with yourself.

To get the full benefits of this workbook you will need to set aside some quiet time to think and reflect on the questions and complete the activities. Each chapter is divided into 3 parts: a summary (useful if you have not read the original book), key takeaways, and exercises.

The exercises will help you to identify your hidden abilities, improve your focus, establish routines, improve relationships, overcome negativity and reduce stress. Learning to think like a monk and apply their ancient wisdom to busy lives can be very challenging. This workbook hopes to assist you in this journey.

If you are looking for a way to add more gratitude, purpose, and joy to your life then the teachings summarised in this workbook, together with the exercises will help take you on a journey of self-exploration. You will learn to train your mind to think like a monk and remain centered and balanced despite the chaos that life sometimes throws at us.

Monks have the most focused and calmest minds and thinking like them helps us to reflect and make our lives more purposeful.

More on Jay

Jay Shetty is a well-known motivational speaker and social media star who spent some time serving as a monk in India. Over the years, his #1 podcast On Purpose, has become a favorite to millions of viewers worldwide. In his podcast, Jay offers practical steps, to live a more meaningful, less anxious life.

Jay bases his advice on the wisdom and lessons he learned while experiencing life as a Vedic monk in Mumbai, India. He has this ability to take ancient wisdoms and make them relevant to today's world.

Jay grew up in life with 3 options: be a doctor, a lawyer, or a failure. But he eventually rebelled against the norm after college to find his true purpose whilst living in an ashram for 3 years as a monk. Jay got inspired to think like a monk for the first time at the age of 18 when he was under pressure to make decisions about his future.

Jay's experience of living like a monk changed his way of thinking and looking at life. He realized that a big part of his purpose was to serve. Although Jay found his purpose while living as a monk, he says that we (the readers) "don't have to live like a monk to think like a monk". If you are willing to open your mind to a different set of ideas and a new way of thinking, you can tap into the benefits of thinking like a monk.

According to Jay, you need to make more of a mindset change than a lifestyle change. Thinking like a monk is a mindset that can be applied to the real world to help us to live a successful life. Monks have learned to cut out the "noise", (distractions of daily life), and to live life intentionally.

So start engaging in this way of thinking and living, and see your life blossom with peace, purpose and probably a healthy measure of prosperity thrown in as well.

Part One – Letting Go

Chapter One – Finding Our Identity

Summary

For most of us, our self-image is largely dictated by how we think others see us. Jay begins chapter one of his book by exploring our identities and how we see ourselves.

Often, we take on a role to either impress others, please others, or fit in with others. This role is similar to what Shetty refers to as, method acting. We all do this to a certain degree. We take on different personas for the different roles we play in our lives. Even our efforts at self-improvement are an attempt to reach these imagined ideals. The problem though is that some of us get so caught up in these personas that we tend to lose sight of the real us.

Who are we really?

In trying to live up to how we think others see us, have we lost sight of who we are at our core? Do we try to maintain these personas at the expense of our values? Do we make choices based on our own beliefs or the expectations of others?

We are constantly surrounded by external pressures telling us who or what to be from our early school days. And we try as much as possible to live up to these external pressures. Unfortunately, when we decide to be ourselves, to be more of our authentic selves, we put some of our relationships in jeopardy. For instance, Jay talks about breaking the news to his parents about becoming a monk. This was not easy for them to understand since it deviated from their dreams and expectations for him.

Nevertheless, despite the pressures from societal and cultural norms as well as friends or parents' opinions, Jay stood fast regarding his decision to join the ashram at a possible risk of jeopardizing his relationships. Looking within, knowing what you want, and doing it despite distractions is the first step to building a monk mind. This is what monks do; they clear away anything that distracts them from their core values.

To be able to identify who you are and what shapes your values you must be able to recognize the external influences that shape you. Reflect on these and work on removing them ("clearing the dust") so you can identify your core beliefs. Removing distractions will allow you to focus on what matters most to you. This will allow you to see your true values.

Our values are what define us, drive us, and influence our actions and relationships. They are formed and influenced by several factors: our parents, our education, society, and the media. Very often we end up living the values we grew up with or that are formed by the influences around us.

To get a clear picture of your values, Jay suggests you audit your life by doing the following:

1. Create space and time for reflection

2. Conduct a self-audit:

    a. Look at what you spent most of your time on
    b. Assess the role of social media in your life
    c. Analyze how you spend your money

Doing a self-audit helps you to see what is important to you. For example, what do you spend a large percentage of your time on? Is this because you value this activity above all else? Do you make decisions based on your values? Are your goals driven by your values or by other people, traditions, or the media?

Who do you spend your time with? According to Jay, the people you surround yourself with should fit in with your values. This will help you to stick to them. The values I mean, not stick to the people. But of course, by default if these are the folks who share the same values as you, you'd probably also stick to them too!

Monks aspire to live their lives according to higher values such as gratitude, service, purity of mind, etc. These higher values lead us toward happiness. Lower values such as envy, greed, illusion, etc lead towards anxiety and depression. Once we have filtered out all the noise and distractions that distort who we truly are, we can begin to direct our lives towards higher values.

Key Insights from this Chapter

1. Who am I? A large part of our identity is distorted by how we think others see us.

2. We are driven by our values, which play a large role in forming our identities.

3. Identifying your true values and letting go of false values will help you discover your true self.

4. Live life on your own terms, not based on other people's opinions.

Identify Related Issues

1. Do you know what your values are? Are you aware of how your values were formed/shaped?

2. Are they your own authentic values?

3. Do you live your life based on your true values or on how you think others see you?

Goals You Want to Achieve

1. Know and live my true values

2. Aspire to higher values and avoid lower values

    Examples of monk values:
    Higher - *Service, compassion, deep study, integrity, gratitude, charity, nonviolence, truthfulness, purity of mind*
    Lower - *greed, anger, illusion, lust, ego, envy*

Your Plan of Action

1. In the table on the next page, write down some of the values that have shaped your life from early childhood to now.

2. Next, write down their origins. Do these values align with your true self?

Value	Origin	Does it align with my true self?
1.Example: Compassion	Parents and Community	Yes
2.Example: Appearance	Social Media	Not really, not any more **or** yes, this is very important to me
3.Example: Competitiveness	School	
4.Example: Material Success	Society	

3. Do your goals, decisions and choices relate to your values?

4. Make a note of what changes you can make to ensure you live a life aligned with your values.

Value	Origin	Does it align with my true self?
1.		
2.		

3.		
4.		
5.		
6.		
7.		
8.		
9.		
10.		

Action Checklist

1. Clear the dust – start to remove anything that distracts you from your core values. This is the first step to building a monk mind.

2. To do this you have to conduct a self-audit:

   a. Who do you spend the most time with? Do they align most closely with your values?

   b. What do you spend your money on and do these things correspond with your values?

   c. Does the time you spend on any media match your values?

3. Let go of O.E.O.s. – start living life on your own terms, not based on other people's Opinions, Expectations, and Obligations.

Chapter Two – Reducing Negativity

Summary

We live in a world surrounded by negativity. It is inevitable and we encounter it in various forms throughout our day. We complain, we criticize, we gossip, we hear bad news on the radio or we just think negative thoughts about people or situations.

Very often negativity comes from within us, as a result of our fears, feelings of insecurity, hurt, or loss. We have 3 core needs; peace, love, and understanding. When one of these is threatened, negativity sometimes arises.

Bad things happen in life, bad things happen to us all, however, we need to move away from the victim mentality. Negativity is contagious. A victim mindset (life is unfair), leads to selfish attitudes and a sense of entitlement. When we are constantly surrounded by negativity, we start to see the world from that negative mindset, we become suspicious of others and we complain more. Complaining and criticizing are also contagious.

We become so used to negative behaviors around us that we don't even realize it.

Weed Out Negativity

We must learn to identify negative people (complainers, critics, competitors, etc) and behaviors and step away from them. In the ashram where Jay served and trained with other monks, the young monks often had to remind themselves not to nurture negative thoughts about others.

The monk way to reverse external negativity is to become an objective observer – through **detachment**. Let go of negative thoughts and feelings. Step away or detach yourself from the emotional situation and try to understand instead of judging. it When you are more aware of the why; when you understand, you can better deal with negative energy.

Try to surround yourself with uplifting people, at least 3 for every negative person in your life. Jay refers to this as the 25/75 principle. Being in the company of happier people, people with good habits, people who are encouraging or inspiring pushes you to grow. If you can't remove negative people from your life then limit the amount of time you give to them.

We cannot get away from all negativity all the time, but we can learn to understand its cause and be mindful of how we deal with it.

Manage Your Negative Thoughts

Once you have learned how to recognize and handle external negativities the next step is to work on reversing internal negativity. Internal negativity comes in the form of envy of others, jealousy, pride, anger, competition, and so on. We need to be able to let go of our negativity or at the very least, learn to manage it. This will put us in a position of having a more positive mindset.

It is not always possible to let go of our negative feelings and thoughts, but we can become aware of them to do something about them.

To purify their thoughts, monks become **aware** of the negative feeling or issue first. Then they pause to consider what it is and where it comes from. And after understanding what it is, they **address** the issue by **amending** their behavior, finding a new way to process the feeling.

Jay calls this process the "SPOT, STOP, SWAP" method. To become aware of negativity means you must learn to SPOT your negative thoughts so you can work towards freeing yourself from them. Learn to identify the origins of your negative thoughts or feelings. Keep in mind that your negative judgments or projections often reflect your own insecurities.

When you are better able to understand the causes of your negativity you can begin to address it – STOP. You need to learn to silence your negativity. Start by releasing your breath and unclenching those tight jaws. Next, be aware of limiting your negative talk; complain less, criticize less, compare less.

In some instances, if you cannot stop, try to SWAP. So, for example, instead of saying, I am not good at this, say I am not good at it yet. Swapping your negativity means trying to amend it. For example, if you must complain, do so mindfully. Thoughtless venting only makes things worse. By being specific about why we are unhappy and choosing what we say carefully, our complaints can be better understood.

Managing and minimizing negativity related to complaining, envy, and gossip is easier than dealing with negative emotions like anger or pain. Anger is one of the biggest negative emotions we need to learn to deal with. The anger we feel towards others takes a huge toll on us. Sometimes one can be in so much pain from anger that the only thing one sees is revenge. But revenge can often backfire. Jay says that if you can rise above revenge, you will be able to start the process of forgiveness.

Practice Forgiveness

There are different levels of forgiveness and one should aim for the highest level which is transformational forgiveness. This is when you can forgive without expecting an apology or anything else in return.

Being able to forgive brings peace of mind and eases stress and anger. Forgiveness though is a two-way street; we must be able to receive and also give forgiveness. We must learn to admit when we are at fault and take responsibility. Forgiving also includes the ability to forgive ourselves.

As we grow, we realize that we sometimes did things in the past that no longer reflect our values now. We feel guilty or ashamed of past actions. We all make mistakes and we cannot undo our past, but we can learn from our mistakes and move on. We must learn to forgive ourselves because sometimes we did the best we could at that time.

To be able to achieve true sattva (goodness and peace) we must be able to, not only forgive the person who caused us pain but to wish them well so both can move on and heal. This will allow you to truly let go.

Key Insights from this Chapter

1. Negativity is not part of a person's identity – you can learn to let it go.

2. Understanding the origins of negativity in your life will help to uproot and manage it.

3. To release ourselves from angry and negative thoughts we need to practice forgiveness.

Identify Related Issues

1. Do you find yourself spending too much energy on negative thoughts?

2. Do you think you need to include less negativity and more positivity in your life? Before you go saying of course, that is a dumb question, be honest and think through carefully. Sometimes we are so caught up in mundane affairs that we lose sight of our core. Take some time to reflect and think through for this portion.

3. Are there any people in your life you need to forgive?

4. Reflecting on your past, can you think of any past mistakes you need to forgive yourself for?

Goals You Want to Achieve

1. Reduce the negative remarks I make and/or thoughts I have, starting with one week. (you will resolve to reduce negativity for that week, via thoughts and remarks. This means you need to be mindful) Then

progressing to one month and beyond. See the impact that reducing negative comments and thoughts have. Reflect on it before you go to bed.

2. The 25/75 principle – for every negative person in my life, I want to have at least 3 uplifting people.

3. Achieve peace of mind through forgiveness.

Your Plan of Action

1. Keep a conscious count of the negative remarks you make over a week. Try to reduce this number in the next week. It doesn't matter if you find the number to be high. Always remember there is a plateau after a climb, and then descent will follow.

2. Spend less time with negative people. Find more happy, positive people to spend time with. Sometimes, spending time doesn't necessarily need to involve any activities. You can just be in the same space at the same time, and bask in comfortable silence. Else you can meditate together too.

3. Practice forgiveness to achieve peace of mind.

Action Checklist

1. Change and manage negativity. Try the following technique:
   Spot – observe, become aware of your negativity (spot your negative thought or feeling)
   Stop – reflect and address the issues (pause and consider why you feel like this or think this)
   Swap – amend/modify your negative behaviour or feeling (change it into a positive)

2. Write a forgiveness letter to yourself.

3. Practice forgiving people in your mind during your meditation practice.

4. You can try this out. Repeat softly to yourself or repeat mentally in your mind. "May all beings be well and happy." Exude feelings of love, compassion and gratitude and you may find yourself feeling better after this practice.

Chapter Three – Managing Fear

Summary

In chapter two Shetty mentions that negativity can often arise from fear. Fear and anxiety are two things that often cause us to lose connection with our abilities. From childhood, we are taught that fear is a negative emotion. We all live with fear but it is what we do with our fear that matters.

We can use our fear to motivate us, to propel us into finding solutions to problems, or we can let our fears overwhelm us and keep us from doing things. To let go of the fears that hold us back, we must learn to find the root causes of our fear. What are you really scared of? For Jay, several of his fears stemmed from his original root fear of not being able to make his parents happy.

Often, we hide our deepest fears from ourselves because it makes us uncomfortable. But by digging deep down, you can work your way past the branches of your fear to find the root and origin so you can deal with it. During his three years as a monk, Shetty says he learned to let go of his fear of *fear*. He is now able to recognize the opportunities that fear presents.

Once we can recognize what fear can teach us then we can use it to learn more about ourselves, our values, and our purpose.

Fear can help us identify what does not serve us. The stresses and challenges that often accompany the fear of change for instance can make us stronger or more productive. When we realize that we can deal with fear, it makes us more confident to be able to handle it in the future.

Learning how to deal with fear means we must change our attitude towards it. We must learn to see what it has to offer us, what can we learn from it. Here are the steps you can take to change your fear from a negative to a positive:

1. Accept your fear – acknowledge and accept that your fear and pain are present.
2. Find fear patterns - identify the situations in which your fear emerges and how you distract yourself from it.
3. The cause of fear – identify the root cause of your fear and find out why you are so closely attached to it.
4. Detaching your fear – a monk mind detaches from fear by focusing on what you can control. Once you have identified your fear and can detach yourself from it, you can begin to minimize it.

When you can look at your fears more objectively, you will be able to address them and manage them. Here are some strategies that can help you to deal with fear:

• Short-circuit the panic that often accompanies short-term fear by focusing on your breathing.

- See the broader picture, not just the current situation to get a wider perspective that helps to deal with fear. Say for example you have a long running fear of being poor despite being reasonably well off in the present, you can focus on the fact that if we delve deep enough, in the end all things are transient, and wealth in itself does not bring about true fulfilment.
- Do not deny long-term fears by burying them or trying to run away from them. Fear and problems related to fear tend to accumulate if we deny them. We need to learn to face our fears to be able to deal with them.
- Use your fear to motivate you towards what you want, not to limit you.

Fear is a normal emotion that we have, but we need to try not to let it control us. Detaching yourself from your fear will help you learn to control it.

Key Insights from this Chapter

1. Many of us let our fears hold us back from what we can truly achieve.

2. Fear can either be used to motivate us or it can overwhelm us.

3. Finding the root causes of our fear and facing it can help us to move past it.

Identify Related Issues

1. Do you have any fears that you have kept hidden?

2. Have you let go of your past fears or do you still carry them with you?

3. Do any of your past fears, pain, or anxieties keep you from doing what you need to do in the present?

4. Can you identify the roots of your fear?

5. Do you want to learn how to let go of or work around these fears? Letting go means to put it away whilst working around the fears can sometimes mean actually harnessing the fear to propel you towards greater heights. For example if someone fears being poor, he or she may do their best to strive in their careers to achieve their desired measure of economic success.

Goals You Want to Achieve

1. Identify my hidden fears or fear patterns.

2. Trace my fears back to their roots.

3. Learn to work with/let go of my fears.

Your Plan of Action

1. Reflect on what you are really scared of. Recognize your fear.

2. Acknowledge and accept your fear/fears.

3. Change your relationship with fear and how you view it. (Monk mind = detachment from fear)

Action Checklist

1. Deal with short-term fears like anxiety or panic by focusing on your breath.
   (For breathwork exercises refer to the end of chapter 4).

2. Identify your deepest fears. Write them down. Which is your worst fear?

3. Next to your fear/s, write down where or how they started.

4. Detach yourself from your fear and reflect on how you can use it to motivate you.

Chapter Four – Living Intentionally

Summary

We have four primary motivators of which fear is one. We can use these four motivators to build a fulfilling life. We all have certain things we want in life and our motivators drive us towards achieving these ambitions. But do we know what exactly motivates each of us?

According to Hindu philosopher, Bhaktivinoda Thakura, four fundamental motivators drive everything we do:

1. Fear – fear of sickness, of poverty, of hell or death
2. Desire – wanting pleasure or wealth or success
3. Duty – gratitude, responsibility, wanting to do the right thing
4. Love – our feelings for others compel us to care for them or help them

Many of the choices we make in life are influenced to a large extent by these four motivators. For example, the fear of getting fired may motivate you to work harder or learn more. Fear as a motivator though is not sustainable in the long term.

The second motivator, desire often takes the form of personal gratification and material goals. Success to many people seems to be the acquiring of things and achievements to reach a state of happiness. The idea that success equals happiness though is an illusion (maya in Sanskrit). Happiness does not come from "external measures of success". Happiness is within us; it is internal while material gratification is external. You can be successful, achieve accolades, wealth, and respect but success does not guarantee happiness.

If fear and desire do not sustainably motivate or satisfy us then perhaps duty and love will. For monks, happiness is not the goal, but living a meaningful life is. Seeing meaning and finding purpose in your actions leads to contentment. Doing things out of love and duty instead of trying to find happiness through success, allows us to achieve more.

When we live with a clear sense of **why** what we do matters, life takes on more meaning and fulfillment. Our intention is what we do or plan to be to help us reach our goals with purpose and meaning. For example, as the eldest sibling in your family, if you are motivated by duty, your intention might be to help your younger siblings no matter how busy you are.

We have different intentions for different motivations, but to live intentionally we must focus on the *why* behind the want. Ask yourself why you want/desire need xxx and keep digging until you get to your true intention. The next step is to live your intention and to do that you have to take certain actions.

Your intentions reveal your values and permeate your behavior. When you get what you want, but you are not happy it is because you did not do it with the right intention. We often find that if we do what we do with the **intention of serving** we begin to find more meaning and purpose.

Breathwork

Jay recommends we do breathwork, focusing on controlled breathing, to look within ourselves. Your breathing tends to change with your emotions. For example, have you noticed that when you are concentrating hard, you hold your breath?

Focused breathing helps to calm and steady us, giving us space to reflect and evaluate our intentions. Being able to control your breath, helps you to control your emotions. Doing breathwork exercises helps you to be more focused and centers you.

Basically you need to be aware of how you are breathing and then start with noticing your breath. You may wish to focus on a point where the breath enters in and out of your nose. Many folks find that concentrating on the spot below the nostrils and above the upper lip is great for noting the entry and exit of the breath.

When you breath in, note that you are breathing in. When you breath out, note that you are breathing out. Attempt at all times to remain focused on the breath and to block out all distracting, wandering thoughts. When any of these thoughts occur, just bring your mind and attention back to the breath.

You may find that you can only do this for a few seconds before wandering thoughts occur. Take heart, it is common as our monkey mind has been jumping around stimuli after stimuli for pretty much the whole of our lives. You will realize that you can slowly extend the period of concentration from a few seconds to a few minutes. From a few minutes to tens of minutes and then gradually evolving to hours.

Work on this and you will realize how much calm and peace it can bring for you.

Key Insights from this Chapter

1. Four primary motivators influence the choices we make: Fear, Desire, Duty, Love.

2. These motivators are the roots of all our intentions. (Our Why behind the Want).

3. When we define ourselves by our intentions, not by our achievements then we can live a truly meaningful life.

4. Happiness comes from within.

Identify Related Issues

1. What do you truly want? What are your desires?

2. **Why** do you want what you want? What are the **intentions** behind your desires?

3. Do you define yourself by your intentions or by your achievements/career?

4. Are you living your intentions? If not, **why** not?

Goals You Want to Achieve

1. To identify my intentions, for example, do I want to help people/do I want to support my family?

2. To take action to live according to my (good) intentions.

Your Plan of Action

1. Identify all your wants and desires. Write them down so they become more tangible. You will find that just inking them down can sometimes trigger certain insights and allows you to form new ideas.

2. Recognize **why** you want what you want. (Identify the **root** of your intention)

3. Plan what you need to do and be to achieve your goals.

Action Checklist

1. Make a list of goals that align with your intentions.

2. Look for role models who live the intentions you wish to live. How do they do that?

3. Make a to-do list and a to-be list (what you need to be to achieve what you want to do, for example, I want to improve my relationship with my partner. To do this, I need to be more understanding/be a better listener). You can be as thorough as you want, but do not have to be daunted by the to-be list if that appears to be long. Many a time you can find common core values running through that list which makes you a better person, and you can just condense it into concepts or precepts with which to better guide your life. Example: you resolve not to take any life, be it however small. (insects included). You may also resolve not to tell lies, verbal or written. (white lies included). These precepts can become guiding posts for your actions and speech in your quest to become a better person. Breaching them does not mean the world has come to an end. Breaching them is akin to you falling down whilst walking along the mountain path. Pick yourself up, dust yourself off, and then resolve to keep your precepts again without breaking them.

4. Consciously align your behavior with your goal to live intentionally. Use meditation and breathwork to help you look within and remove distractions. You can fit meditation into your daily life. It doesn't have to be daunting, a simple 10 or 15 minute session can lay the foundation for longer sessions in the future.

Part Two – Grow

Chapter Five – Finding Your Purpose

Summary

In part one we learned that letting go of distractions and detaching from our fears and negativity helps us to open our minds. Now in part two, we focus on our growth. To find our purpose and our passion we begin by exploring our strengths and weaknesses.

In the ashram, the monks learn how to connect to their *dharma*. Dharma is a Sanskrit word that does not have a direct translation in English. It can best be described as your calling. According to Jay, "when your natural talents and passions (your *varna*) connect with what the universe needs (*seva*) and become your purpose, you are living your dharma". *Seva* is what monks strive for, that is, to selflessly serve others.

When you live your dharma, you are moving towards living a life of fulfillment. To grow and live your life according to your values and intentions you need to begin with dharma. The more faith you have in your dharma, the harder you will be willing to work to fulfill it.

Discovering your Dharma

We all have a natural inclination to lean towards the things we are good at. Dharma is when we use what we are good at, what we have a passion for, to serve others. When we receive a positive response, it shows us that our passion has purpose. And when our passion has purpose, it makes us happy. Jay

passion + expertise + usefulness = dharma

proposes that the "magic formula" for dharma is:

Your passion and your purpose are already within you. Your dharma is already a part of your being and just needs to be discovered. Keeping an open and curious mind will eventually lead you to your dharma.

Nowadays the pressure to achieve as early as possible causes a lot of stress and anxiety in many people. Although some find their passion and purpose early in life, others are late bloomers. Many successful people only discover their dharma later in life and that's okay.

Whether you discover your dharma early in life or later, the important thing is to ensure you are pursuing your **own** dharma. Do not live the life somebody else wants for you as Andre Agassi did. He became a great tennis star because he was pushed into it by his dad. It is only now after retiring from tennis that he has found his true passion which is to serve others through the Andre Agassi Foundation.

In discovering and following our dharmas we tend to lean on our strengths, but we should also develop our weaknesses. Sometimes a skill we think we are weak at may connect to our dharma in some way. This happened to Jay who disliked public speaking when he was young but later discovered it connected to his dharma. In serving others after finding his true purpose, he has had to call on the public speaking skills he was forced to learn as a youngster.

Our dharmas are not always recognizable and they may not always follow a common path. To reveal our dharmas we must first identify our passions. What do we love and are naturally good at doing?

Jay puts forward the idea of the "quadrants of potential". Ideally, we would all like to spend as much time as we can in quadrant two which is doing what we love and are most skilled at. However, not everyone can be where they desire to be. What we can do is to try to eventually move our energy and time towards doing things we are good at and love (Quadrant 2).

Quadrants of Potential:

Quadrant 1 – doing the things we are good at, but don't love (skill, but no passion)

Quadrant 2 – using our time and our talents to do what we love (skill and passion)

Quadrant 3 – spending our time and effort on what we are not good at and don't love (no skill and no passion)

Quadrant 4 – doing what we are not good at, but we love (no skill, but passion)

If you are stuck in quadrant one, then try to at least look for opportunities to do what you love in the life you are already living. For example, you might be an excellent lawyer, but your true passion is to bake and enter a baking show. You might not be able to follow that passion because you need your job and you are good at it. Instead, find a place in your life to include your passion. For instance, bake for your colleagues or your family.

Identifying your Varna

To help you seek out your dharma, identify your varna. According to the Bhagavad Gita, your varna is your personality type. Your varna gives you an idea of what you are good at and what your true nature is. There are four varnas: the Guide, the Leader, the Creator, and the Maker.

Guide – skilled in learning, likes to share knowledge, reflects, works alone. Guides value wisdom more than wealth or fame. Coaches, teachers or mentors.

Leader – engages others, inspiring, works in teams, is organized, focused, dedicated, complements guides. Often found in law enforcement, justice and, politics.

Creator – likes to make things happen, good at persuading others, driven by success and status, hardworking, good in business, good at networking and innovating, dynamic and goal-oriented.

Maker – creative, inventing, maintains work-life balance, values stability, complements creators. Makers make good musicians, artists, engineers, and chefs.

The idea of the varnas like any other personality test you may take is to become aware of your passions and skills. This will lead to a better understanding of yourself.

Embracing your dharma means you must be able to let go of fears, negative beliefs, ego, or self-deceiving ideas that get in the way of your passions. Being in your dharma will enable you to feel alive, stable, calm, excited, in your flow, comforted, energetic, and positive. You will feel more confident in your own abilities and you will want to be in a place in which you thrive. For monks, passion becomes purpose, when used to serve.

Key Insights from this Chapter

1. Discovering and connecting to your dharma can lead you to a more fulfilled and meaningful life.

2. Doing what we are good at and what we love is what we should be aiming towards.

3. When your dharma becomes your purpose, you use your passion to serve others.

Identify Related Issues

1. Are you doing what you love? Are you living your passion? Do you want to?

2. Do you know what is your dharma? What are your varnas?

3. What is your quadrant of potential?

4. How can you use your passion and expertise to serve?

Goals You Want to Achieve

1. Discover my dharma and find my true passion and purpose. You may not find it right off the bat and that is

perfectly alright. Remember to keep and open mind and definitely try new stuff. You might just chance upon it.

2. Live according to my dharma or find ways to fit it into my current life.

Your Plan of Action

1. Identify my passions and my skills (varnas)

2. Look for opportunities to do what I love and am good at in life (Quadrant 2). Be active in the search. You might want to spend maybe 1 or 2 hours each day just to make this happen. Usually it may involve a little thinking and retrospection at the start, for you will want to reflect and think through what you are good at, as well as the stuff that you love to do. If any of it overlaps, those are the areas which you will want to pay attention to.

3. Embrace my dharma in all aspects of my life

Action Checklist

1. To find out which varna (Vedic personality type) is your primary one, take this online survey: https://s.surveyanyplace.com/dharmatype

2. Identify your quadrant of potential. Which of the quadrants would you place yourself in right now?

3. How close are you to living your dharma at present? Answer the questions below to find out:

   a. Do you like your job?

   b. Are you good at your job?

   c. Do you have a passion outside of your current job?

   d. If your passion is not part of your job, can you find a way to include it or can you find a way to bring it into your life in another way? Write down your ideas for how you can do this.

Chapter Six – The Value of Routine

<u>Summary</u>

If you use your time and energy wisely, living according to your dharma will be productive. It is important to begin each new day with a fresh start. Ashram mornings start with a routine so simple that it is completely stress-free. Many of us, however, begin our day with mornings full of stress while rushing to get things done.

This is the morning routine most people tend to follow; can you tick off any of these?

Wake up to an alarm clock

Wake up tired after getting too little sleep

Reach for your cell phone within minutes of opening your eyes

Check messages or feeds (some of which may cause anxiety or stress)

Rush to get showered and dressed

Skip breakfast/stand-up breakfast/pack lunches/sort out kids for school

Traffic!

Jay says that to do anything with purpose you cannot speed through things. He advises us to wake up an hour earlier to avoid the morning rush and high stress. **How we begin our day sets the tone for the rest of the day**. Many successful people start their day early; before 4 am for some (Richard Branson, Michelle Obama, Tim Cook, Jeff Bezos are all early risers).

Waking up an hour earlier means you should get to bed earlier to ensure you have enough hours of sleep. You don't have to wake up at 4 am; start small. Even if you create 15 extra minutes in the morning it can make a difference. Giving yourself some extra (free) time in the morning allows you to move more intentionally. You can use this extra time to exercise, meditate, reflect, enjoy your coffee or go through your morning chores without rushing.

To wake up earlier, you should go to bed earlier. Instead of snoozing on the couch or watching TV because you are too tired to move, head off to bed. To establish a good morning routine, you should start with having a good, restful evening routine. There are things you can do the evening before to make your mornings less stressful. Jay suggests figuring out what you want to do first the next day, before going to sleep.

Removing challenges such as deciding what to wear every morning also helps. He suggests finding your version of a monk's robe. Simplify your choices. Establish routines. Certainly Apple's late CEO Steve Jobs springs to mind when we touch on simplified wardrobe choices.

When you do certain things out of routine, it leaves your mind free to discover new things; to be open to creativity and spontaneity. If you have an established routine, it is good to look for something new or different or simply from a different perspective. This will allow you to find value in your routine or daily activities, leading to greater appreciation.

Your environment gives off a particular kind of energy and you can either thrive in that energy or not. Develop an awareness of the type of environment you thrive in. Some people prefer quiet and solitude, others thrive in a busy environment. Are you one of those that works better in a cluttered space? Do you like a change of scenery or the familiar?

Be aware of where you are more productive to serve your dharma. You must try not to confuse the energies of a particular space. For instance, your bedroom should be a place for sleep, not to work in or eat in. Bedrooms should be a place of calm with few distractions to make it easier to sleep in.

Once you have identified where you thrive, try to spend more time in that place or a similar space. This will create the kind of energy you need to give attention to your purpose. "Location has energy" – doing something in the same space every day makes it easier and more natural. In the same way, doing something at the same time every day becomes easier and more natural. It becomes a habit. "Time Has memory."

Studies have found that to be wholly present in a moment, you need to single-task. Many people believe they can multitask effectively, but this is not necessarily true. Only 2% of the population can multitask; most are not effective at it. It is better to keep your brain focused on one thing at a time. Studies show that periods of deep focus are better for your brain than switching tasks compulsively.

Jay says that monks do things "immersively". They experience/do each thing in a fully focused state before moving on to the next thing. While this may not always be possible in a world away from the ashram, one should at least try it, especially for important things.

Key Insights from this Chapter

1. Use your time and energy wisely; begin each morning with a fresh start to reduce anxiety and stress.

2. Reclaim sleep; ensuring you get a full night's rest will improve the quality of your productivity the next day.

3. To be wholly present in the moment and fully focused on your tasks it is better to practice single-tasking as opposed to multitasking.

Identify Related Issues

1. How do you start your morning? Is it relaxed or rushed and stressful?

2. Does your morning consist of an organized structure?

3. Do you get enough sleep? Is it of good quality or do you toss and turn at night?

4. Are you a certified multi-tasker? If so, how is that working out for you?

Goals You Want to Achieve

1. Create a more effective morning and evening routine.

2. Appreciate my everyday activities and become more aware of what I do.

Your Plan of Action

1. Wake up earlier and start my day off on a positive note

2. Change my morning routine to be less rushed/less stressful

3. Try to get more sleep and more quality sleep

4. Go to sleep with good thoughts.

5. Set my intentions for the morning, the night before

6. Consciously find value in mundane tasks

7. Practice like what the monks do and be immersed in which ever task or project you are doing. For example, if you are washing plates, be focused on that activity. Be mindful of the water running down your hands, be aware of how you are scrubbing the plates clean and wiping them dry. Any time you find your mind starting to wander and think about that favorite sitcom, bring it back to the task at hand.

Action Checklist

1. Try to integrate TIME into your morning routine:

   a. **T** – Thankfulness (expressing gratitude)
   b. **I** – Insight (read or listen to something uplifting)
   c. **M** – Meditation (spend some quiet alone time doing breathwork)
   d. **E** – Exercise (Do some basic stretches, yoga, or a morning workout)

2. Take some time before going to bed tonight to jot down 3 things you want to achieve tomorrow morning.

3. Start cutting down on multitasking and learn to fully focus on one task at a time. Practice single-tasking.

4. Engage in that single task with mindfulness. Be aware of the present and how you are performing that task.

Chapter Seven – Train the Mind

Summary

In this chapter, we delve into the workings of our minds. The human mind is in constant motion. We are continuously thinking; not necessarily about the present moment but backwards and forwards, always anticipating and guessing what's going to happen next.

According to the Buddha "the wise shape their minds" and Jay says that "true growth requires understanding the mind". Every day each of us wages a battle in our minds about the choices we make; from the smallest of choices to bigger ones. Should I wear this shirt today or the other? Do I send in my resignation letter today or wait another month?

Sometimes our minds work against us (inner conflict) and we end up doing things we regret. We need to learn that "we are not our minds". If we see our minds as a separate entity to us, we can then improve our relationship with it.

The first step to understanding our minds is to differentiate between "monkey mind" (child) and "monk mind" (adult/parent). Which voice are we hearing inside our heads; the child voice or the adult voice? The child mind is more spontaneous than the adult mind, it is creative and dynamic and gets frustrated more easily. The adult mind assesses the bigger picture and weighs up options. But the adult voice can only take over if it is well trained and has self-control.

Sorting out the conflict in our heads is not as easy as it may seem because we are constantly weighing input from several sources:

- Our five senses – responsible for our wants, likes, passions, and impulses
- Our intellect – processing and evaluating
- Our memories – recalling past experiences

To master our senses, we must learn to calm the mind. This is what monks do. Shaolin monks train their minds to achieve sensory control through vigorous training, meditation, and breathing techniques. Jay says that because the monkey mind is reactive, we need to learn to steer our senses away from stimuli that can trigger it (temptations). Removing some of the unwanted mental or physical triggers can stop us from giving in to them.

To do this, we must gain self-control. An important tool that monks use to gain self-control is **meditation**. Meditation allows us to "regulate sensory input". Another way to train the mind is to build the relationship between the adult mind and the child mind so that they collaborate.

For us to reach this kind of collaboration, our minds need to pay close attention to our subconscious. Our subconscious minds are programmed to follow the same paths we have always used before. To change these thoughts, beliefs, and behaviors we must actively wake up our subconscious (See Activity 1 under Action Checklist below) and get rid of self-defeating thoughts.

To rid ourselves of self-defeating thoughts we must rewire our mindset and we can do this by talking to ourselves. Talking out loud to yourself and even using your own name while doing so is a powerful way of grabbing your attention and getting you to focus. Researchers also found that talking to yourself helps to boost your memory and concentration.

In addition to talking to ourselves, Jay proposes other ways we can shift our mindset:

• **Reframing** self-criticism and unwanted thoughts in terms of knowledge by identifying how you are making progress. For example, instead of saying I am bad at this, say I can get better at this by…. Turn your negative thoughts into a positive "solution-oriented spin". Another way to reframe your state of mind in terms of knowledge is to learn a new thing every day.

• Slow things down by **writing** down your thoughts especially when you are anxious and your mind is racing with thoughts. Writing helps you to gain a more objective or critical perspective which you can use to find a solution.

- Show yourself some love by responding to negative thoughts with compassion. In other words, according to Jay find **self-compassion**: "treat yourself with the same love and respect you want to show others".

- **Be present** in the moment. We spend too much time thinking about the past or worrying about the future. Being trapped in the past closes us off from new experiences. We cannot change the past and we cannot know the future. Planning for the future is always a good idea but we should not let it cause us too much anxiety or unnecessary worry.

- **Detachment** – step away from the emotion or out of the situation. Being able to detach is a form of self-control that monks practice. Decrease also the number of things you are attached to. Jay says "nothing should own you".

When you can open your mind to new possibilities and detach from thoughts that limit you, you will find that you are capable of so much more.

To fully detach from something, you must first be aware of its attachment to you, like for example social media. How much time do you dedicate to social media daily? Do you want to limit this time? If so, you can do it the monk way, which is more extreme, and give it up cold turkey for a month. Alternatively, you can make small, gradual changes starting with giving it up one evening a week and so on.

Over time, you will begin to see the benefits of detachment, you will feel more confident and you will gain control over the monkey mind.

Key Insights from this Chapter

1. Understanding and training the mind allows true growth to take place.

2. Differentiating between the monkey mind and the monk mind helps sort out the conflict in our heads.

3. To master our senses, we must learn to calm our minds. Self-control and detachment help with this.

4. A shift in mindset will help us to get rid of self-defeating thoughts.

Identify Related Issues

1. Do I have a calm mind? Am I in control of my senses or do they control me?

2. What self-defeating thoughts do I have? What can I do about my self-defeating thoughts?

Goals You Want to Achieve

1. Rewire my mindset to get rid of my self-defeating thoughts and/or attachments.

2. Treat myself with the same love and respect I show to others.

Your Plan of Action

1. Acknowledge and write down my self-defeating thoughts and reframe them.

2. Make my self-talk less negative and talk to myself with love.

3. Disconnect from limiting ideas or habits by practicing detachment.

Action Checklist

1. Wake up your subconscious. Write down any negative self-defeating thoughts your mind sends you daily. For example: You can't do this or you don't have the ability to do this or you are not lovable enough or you are not smart enough.

2. Reframe the negative thoughts created by the monkey mind into solution-oriented thoughts such as: I am not

good at this, but I am taking steps to learn how to become better at it.

3. Identify the negative things you say to yourself. Write them down. Would you say this to someone else? How could you present it in a kinder, more loving way?

4. What are you attached to? Does it make you vulnerable in any way? Are you addicted? Try taking something you are attached to and see if you can detach yourself from it over the next week. Either swap in new behaviour or limit it. Start by making a small change, then gradually build on it.

Chapter Eight - The Ego

<u>Summary</u>

Our egos have a huge influence on our minds and can sometimes be an obstacle to how open we are to learning. When we are humble, we understand how much we don't know, unlike the 'know-it-all'. According to the Bhagavad Gita, there is a clear distinction between the ego and the false ego.

The ego (real ego) is our consciousness, it makes us who we are. The false ego is the know-it-all; it is an identity we use to make us seem the best. An unchecked false ego hides our true natures. The persona we present to the public is not the same as the person we are at home. We want others to perceive us as more than we are.

Why do we present a more polished self to the world? This is usually due to pride, vanity, and ego. Jay says that if you are satisfied with who you are, you do not need to impress others or prove your worth to others. *Who are you when no one is watching?* That is the true you.

When our false ego takes over, it wants to impress others. Sometimes it compels us to lie because we want to be perceived as more than what we are or know. This ego craves praise and recognition. Our real egos are really our healthy self-image which emerges when we live our dharma.

False egos also put other people down, ranking people according to their appearance and material positions and discriminating according to physical attributes. The false or arrogant ego desires respect, but humility inspires respect. Monks treat everyone with equal honor and respect; status or worth does not matter to them. When we judge or criticize others it is a projection of our own shortcomings or insecurities.

Shetty says that all this pretense to be someone we are not (false egos) is an obstacle to our growth. We fail to listen to others and learn because we are too busy thinking about what we want to say. After all, why listen when you know it all already. This limits our opportunities to learn or see things from a different perspective. It restricts our ability to be open-minded and in turn our opportunities for growth and change.

Humility

When an inflated ego breaks, it results in low self-esteem. But sometimes a deflated ego can show you who you truly are, bringing about much-needed humility. Humility is a balance between the highly inflated ego and low self-esteem. Being humble teaches us that we can be good at some things and imperfect in others. We learn to understand our weaknesses through humility.

In the ashram, Jay learned to practice humility through doing simple and menial tasks. They were also taught that if you remember the bad you have done to others your ego is forced to acknowledge its imperfections. Remembering the good others have done for us makes us feel humbled and grateful.

While it is good to remember, it is also good to forget. We should forget the good we have done for others and the bad that others have done to us. This is because being impressed by own good deeds grows our egos. And harboring grudges and anger towards those that have done bad to us keeps us focused on ourselves.

Keep that ego in check

Become more aware when your ego flares up and try not to indulge it. Repressing your ego will limit its power over you. Here are a few actions you can take to keep your ego in check:

Detachment

To quiet your ego in a specific situation, detach from the reaction; become an objective observer. Remember that you are not defined by your accomplishments; you don't have to be the best. Detaching makes us realize that we should be grateful for all who helped us achieve and not let our accomplishments get to our heads.

Accept where you are

Understand that where you are currently is not necessarily a reflection of who you are. If you feel that you are not where you want to be in terms of your career or success, do not see yourself as a failure. This is your ego talking, not you.

Build confidence

There is a difference between ego and a healthy self-esteem. The ego wants everyone to like you, it knows everything and always wants to prove itself. A healthy self-esteem does not compare to others, it can learn from others and respects self and others. A healthy self-esteem does not worry about what people will say, it can filter what people say and uses this to build self-confidence.

Accumulate small wins

When we celebrate our small wins, we build up confidence. Break your goals up into more achievable short-term goals.

Seek feedback

Cultivate people around your specific areas of interest, work, etc whom you can ask for advice. To get productive feedback, look for your *guru*, as the monks do. A guru is someone who has the knowledge to guide you. Find a trusted source who wants the best for you always.

Filter feedback

Be alert to feedback from others; this can be in the form of non-verbal feedback. Be aware of how others react to you. The ego tends to write off feedback as criticism, but you should learn to reflect on feedback. Evaluating and responding to feedback helps you to make improvements.

Don't let your achievements go to your head

Remember to practice **gratitude** for the people in your life that have taught you, guided you, and helped you along the way and for all you have been given. Being gracious will keep you grounded and humble.

Keep moving your goalposts

No matter what you achieve, you can still aspire to go further. Jay says that "real greatness is when you use your own achievements to teach others". Aim beyond yourself towards your community, your country, and the planet. Realizing that the "ultimate" goal is somewhat unattainable will keep us humble.

Incorporating Visualisation into your Meditation Practice

Monks use the power of visualization for the mind to transform how they see themselves. Visualization is a great technique to use to help you heal the past and prepare for the future.

During meditation, two types of visualization can be practiced. In the first type, "set visualization" you are guided verbally by another person providing all the details of a place. The second type, "exploratory visualization" does not involve an external narrator; you come up with your own details. Think about a place where you feel most at ease.

Visualization allows you to draw the energy from a past or future situation to bring it into your reality. Remember to visualize positive things, not negative things.

Key Insights from this Chapter

1. When we think we are a know-it-all it becomes an obstacle to our learning.

2. An unchecked ego becomes inflated and limits our opportunities to grow.

3. A healthy ego reflects our true self and encourages humility and gratitude.

4. Use visualization to help you heal the past and prepare for the future.

Identify Related Issues

1. Who am I when no one is looking? Am I true to myself?

2. Time for an ego check: do I have an inflated or false ego?

3. Do I practice humility and gratitude?

4. How do I react to feedback?

5. Are there trusted people in my life whose feedback I can rely on?

Goals You Want to Achieve

1. Ensure I have a healthy ego that reflects my true self.

2. Detach from my ego and practice humility and gratitude.

3. Identify my gurus (guides)

Your Plan of Action

1. I will consciously try to keep my ego in check and work on developing a healthy self-esteem instead.

2. I will practice using techniques such as detachment to keep my ego in check.

3. Make a list of trusted sources I can get reliable feedback or advice from and act on the feedback.

Action Checklist

1.

    a) Using this table (see below) tick the statements you believe apply to you.

Ego	✓	Self-esteem	✓
Fears what people will say		Filters what people say	
Compares to others		Compares to themselves	
Wants to prove themselves		Wants to be themselves	
Knows everything		Can learn from anyone	
Pretends to be strong		Is ok being vulnerable	
Wants people to respect them		Respects self & others	

b) If you ticked off anything on the ego side of the table, write down a list of changes you need to make to help you move to the self-esteem side of the table. Start to implement these changes.

2. Big steps aren't needed in order to steer you in the right direction. Remember working on each portion in a step by step manner will benefit you more in the long run. Come up with working details on the list of changes you wish to make and take it bit by bit if you happen to find it daunting in the beginning. However, remember to take action. Small action always beats no action.

Part Three – Give

Chapter Nine – Practice Gratitude

<u>Summary</u>

In part two of this workbook, we learned to train our minds to look inward. In this chapter we look outward; how we interact with other people in the world around us. We will look at how we can practice and express gratitude. Do we appreciate the people in our lives? Do we recognize their value to us?

According to Jay Shetty, scientific research proves that **gratitude is good for you**. Gratitude can be beneficial in lowering your stress levels. One study showed that gratitude journaling helped college students in an experimental group sleep better.

Gratitude helps us to counter the negativity brought forth by the monkey mind. When we feel grateful our brain releases dopamine the "feel good" chemicals in our brain. Gratitude blocks out toxic emotions which in turn has a positive effect on our physical bodies, not just our minds. Some studies show that grateful people feel healthier.

Since gratitude is good for us it makes sense then that increasing gratitude in our daily lives would be beneficial. Monks practice gratitude and appreciation every day. Expressing gratitude becomes a habit once we can recognize what has been given to us and we appreciate it.

Take a few minutes every day to practice gratitude in your daily life. A minute of saying thanks for all you have in life, for the people in your life, etc can be done first thing in the morning or at mealtimes or before going to bed.

Once you are used to practicing gratitude during a particular time, see if you can extend this to being always grateful at different times and situations in your life. Shetty relates this to the "conscious practice of gratitude" which can help alleviate the "poverty mindset" (focus on what we lack) that some people have.

Gratitude can also be found in setbacks that we experience. For example, sometimes a missed job opportunity or a rejection can lead to a different opportunity opening up. Practicing "grateful living" allows you to see "every moment as a gift".

One of the most basic ways we can express gratitude outwardly, i.e., to others is by saying thank you. Shetty says that when **expressing thanks**, you should try to make it as specific as you can. Say why you are grateful. This type of feedback makes a person feel even better.

According to the teachings of the Buddha, kindness and gratitude go hand in hand. They work together. Kindness is when you genuinely want something good for someone and you put the effort in giving/doing for them. Kindness inspires gratitude. Remember though when someone expresses gratitude to you, you must be mindful of your ego. When monks are praised, they detach; they receive gratitude with humility. Appreciate the person giving you thanks.

We can practice gratitude in many ways. Being kind to strangers and receiving kindness creates opportunities for gratitude. In serving others, for example by being a volunteer, we can increase our gratitude by appreciating what we have. Research proves that volunteering increases our feelings of well-being and can minimize feelings of depression.

Have you noticed that it is harder to express our gratitude to the people closest to us than it is to others? Has this happened to you? If so, make a conscious effort to change this. Maybe you can start by putting your appreciation and feelings of gratitude into words, write a note, or a short letter. Try to be grateful for the efforts of others; don't only look at what they have failed to do for you.

Key Insights from this Chapter

1. Incorporating gratitude into our daily lives is beneficial to us and others.

2. Take time to consciously practice gratitude and appreciate what you have.

3. Express your gratitude and appreciation for others and be kind. Kindness inspires gratitude.

Identify Related Issues

1. What am I grateful for? Who am I grateful to?

2. Do I show appreciation to the people around me?

3. Is gratitude a part of my daily life?

4. How can I try to incorporate gratitude into my daily life?

Goals You Want to Achieve

1. I want to be more aware of and appreciate things or people in my life that I should be grateful for.

2. I want to consciously practice gratitude and kindness in my life.

3. I want to show the people in my life that I am grateful for them.

Your Plan of Action

1. Make conscious gratitude a part of my daily life. Give thanks every day.

2. Express my gratitude and appreciation for others more often.

3. Volunteer my services wherever I can and where it is needed.

Action Checklist

1. Keep a <u>gratitude journal</u>. Every evening before going to bed, jot down at least five things you are grateful for. Notice if this influences your sleep. After a week note if there has been an improvement in your quality of sleep.

2. Practice gratitude every day: Instead of checking your phone the first thing in the morning when you wake up, take a moment to first reflect on whatever is good in your life. At mealtimes, taking a moment to say thanks for the food and or the people who prepared it is another way of practicing gratitude.

3. Write a gratitude letter to someone in your life to whom you are grateful.

4. Look for groups in your community that are looking for volunteers and offer your skills where they can be useful.

Chapter 10 – Our Relationships

Summary

The ashram in which monks live is like a small village - an interdependent community. Everyone living at the ashram is encouraged to look out for the needs of others and to serve one another.

In his first year of living as a monk at the ashram, Jay found that he was giving out love but not getting it back in return. This was because he assumed that the love he gave out to a specific person would be returned by that person. But one of his teachers told him that love is like a circle – when you give out love, it will come back to you but not always directly from the source it was given to.

Monks believe that the different people in our lives serve different purposes. Each person's role influences our growth in different ways. These roles are not necessarily fixed; your teacher can at some point become your student and so on. Our expectations of others are often tied up in the purpose we allocate for them in our lives.

The people we allow into our lives fall into one of the following four categories:

i.   Competence – We recognize this person as having the skills to solve our issues and we trust their opinions. They usually have expertise or authority in their field. We tend to listen to their advice.

ii.   Care – These are the people in our lives that care the most about our well-being. They believe in us and support us whether we are successful or not in what we do.

iii.   Character – People we trust who have a strong moral background and uncompromising values. We value their opinions and they have good reputations.

iv.   Consistency – These are the people we can always rely on. They have been there for us during our high times and our low times. They are always available when we need them.

These four categories are essentially four types of trust that we instinctively look for in people. It is important to keep in mind that no one person can fulfill all four types. It is unrealistic for us to expect one person to play every role in our life. Different people in our life fulfill these different roles. Nobody can be competent in all four of these things, nor should we expect them to be (not even our partners).

When we are growing up, we come to realize that our families are not necessarily able to fulfill all four of these roles. And that is okay because as Jay says "in order to find diversity, we have to be open to new connections". As he traveled with the monks and connected to diverse groups of people in India and Europe, he started to recognize that everyone was his family in some way or another.

People come and go in our lives for different reasons. Some stay longer than others. But in the end, we learn from each one.

Trust

In every relationship that we build, one of the most essential ingredients is trust. Once we understand what our expectations are for each relationship we have, then it is easier to build trust and to maintain that trust. It is important to keep in mind that trust is about intentions, not abilities.

Trust is earned and we don't trust everyone equally. We trust some people more deeply than others. Our level of trust in a person usually corresponds to our experience with that person. Our level of trust grows in four stages:

•   Neutral trust – this is the first stage; it begins when we first meet a person. At first, we do not trust them which is a normal reaction. They may have some likable characteristics but at this stage we don't trust blindly.

•   Contractual trust – this is a quid pro quo type of trusting relationship. A sort of, 'I will scratch your back if you scratch my back', type of trust. It is a useful type of trust that we usually share with most people whom we come across.

- <u>Mutual Trust</u> – when contractual trust reaches a higher level, this is known as mutual trust. This is where you know that you will be there for one another. Good friends tend to develop this type of trust.

- <u>Pure Trust</u> – this is the highest level of trust in which you both know that no matter what happens you will always be there for each other. Only a handful of people are reserved for this level.

Long-term trust evolves naturally and takes time, patience and commitment. Trust needs to be reinforced and built up daily because it can be threatened in different ways.

Shetty suggests we build and reinforce trust by making promises and fulfilling them to build contractual trust. Build mutual trust by complimenting those you care about and go out of your way to offer them support. When you stand by someone you care for even when they have made a big mistake or when they are in a bad place this shows pure trust.

Romantic Relationships

A relationship we tend to put a lot of energy and effort into is usually our romantic relationship. Monks in embracing celibacy do not have to spend that time and energy on developing and maintaining a romantic relationship. Instead, they focus more on building their relationships with their own selves and developing self-awareness.

What attracts us to other people? Jay puts forward five motivations for why people form connections:

- Physical attraction – their looks, style, and presence draw you to them. You like to be seen with them. They excite you on the physical level.

- Material – you like their possessions, accomplishments, and power

- Intellectual – their conversation and ideas stimulate you

- Emotional – you connect well on an emotional level; they understand your feelings. They seem to instinctively know what you are thinking and can empathize well with you.

- Spiritual – you have similar goals and values

Most people are attracted to their partners through a combination of some of the factors above. Monks believe the first 3 motivators do not build long-term strong relationships on their own. One or both of the last two factors need to be present as well. Emotional and spiritual motivators lead to a deeper, long-term connection.

Another factor that builds good romantic relationships is the energy we expend on a relationship. We should be focusing on quality, not quantity. Spending hours with someone does not mean much if you do not give them your focused full presence while you are with them. Jay puts forward 3 loving exchanges that couples can practice to encourage bonding.

1.   Gifts – give with intention. Put thoughtfulness into giving and receiving. Be grateful for the effort that was put into choosing the gift.

2.   Conversation – one of the best gifts we can give to another is the ability to listen intentionally. Listen to understand without judgment. Remember what was said. Create an atmosphere of trust. Share your own worries and dreams, showing you trust the other person.

3.   Anything that nourishes body or spirit – this can range from experiences to creating food they like, to giving a massage or playing music they like.

All the motivators and exchanges listed above can exist, but without the essential ingredient of love, relationships falter. Learning to understand and love ourselves enables us to be able to love and understand another person.

Another factor to keep in mind is that it is important to keep the love alive. Jay recommends that couples find new ways to spend their time together, explore new things, participate in new activities together, serve together, meditate together, etc to keep the freshness and excitement ongoing in their relationship.

Unfortunately, sometimes we end up in toxic relationships that don't work out. Jay has a few strategies to recover from the heartbreak that results from this. He says that we should use the time after a break-up to assess and make changes. He suggests you learn from the situation and analyze what was good and what was bad. Evaluate your role in the breakup and wait before jumping into another relationship. Take some time to grow, understand yourself, and build your self-esteem before dating again.

Key Insights from this Chapter

1. The different people in our lives serve different purposes or roles. They fall into 1 of 4 categories: competence, care, character, consistency.

2. An essential component in any relationship that we build, is trust, which grows in 4 stages: neutral, contractual, mutual, pure.

3. We are attracted to other people and form relationships with them through a combination of different motivators.

4. The energy you give to a relationship should be focused on quality, not just quantity.

5. Relationships are not perfect and sometimes they may not work out. Getting over heartbreak takes time.

Identify Related Issues

1. What are my expectations regarding the people in my life?

2. Do I expect the people close to me to provide all four roles/types of trust?

3. What do I offer in return? How do I serve them?

4. Do I trust too easily? Who do I trust? Why?

5. Do I spend enough quality time with the people I am close to? Can I do better?

6. Have my partner and I drifted apart? How can we reconnect?

Goals You Want to Achieve

1. Set realistic expectations for what the people in my life can give me.

2. Make more of an effort to spend quality time with the people I care about.

3. Reconnect with my partner to ensure we spend quality time together and our exchanges are intentional.

Your Plan of Action

1. Identify and be grateful for the people in your life whom you trust and who trust you in return.

2. Consciously make an effort to bring your full presence and energy to your engagements with people you care about.

3. Listen attentively with understanding and share your own thoughts honestly with your partner. Make sure you are both are keeping the love alive and growing together.

Action Checklist

1. Reflect on the people you trust in your life. Pick 4 diverse people in your life – a friend, work colleague, relative, etc – and looking at the 4 C's, decide which one they bring into your life. Keep in mind that some people may fill more than one role. You can use the table on the following page for that:

The 4 C's of trust	Relationship to you	Why this category?
Competence		
Care		
Character		
Consistency		

2. Write down what you offer the people in your life in return. How do you serve them? Can you do anything different or more?

3. There are four stages of trust and the different people in our lives usually fall into one of these stages as trust grows stronger.

    a. Reflect on who you trust and which stage you are at with them.

    b. Who do you trust the most, who is part of your 'pure trust' circle? Do you reciprocate this level of trust?

4. Assess whether you bring focused energy and your full attention to your conversations with your loved ones.

Agree with your partner to set some boundaries regarding your phone usage or media time. Focus on reconnecting on your relationship by doing new things together that interest you both. Engage in loving exchanges.

Chapter 11 – Service Mindset

<u>Summary</u>

Jay Shetty says that the most important lesson he learned as a monk is that the highest purpose in life is **to serve**. Everything around us is here to serve. For instance, in nature, the sun provides us with warmth, plants provide us with oxygen and trees provide us with shelter. To be one with nature, one must serve.

Even though monks have already dedicated their life to service they still believe they can give more, i.e., to "seek a higher level of service". We too should try to serve as best we can. We can do this by serving others. To do this in a fulfilling manner, we should try to serve within our dharmas.

Shetty acknowledges that given the pressures we are under (work, family, etc), many people are resistant to this idea. He says that many of us may want to help others and some of us do find ways to help, but how many of us live a life where selflessness is central?

To think like a monk means to serve because that is the life monks live. We cannot all live like monks, because, we need to earn a living. But in adopting a **service mindset**, we can look at what we have and see how we can use what we have, to serve.

Money and resources can be used to support causes. We can volunteer our time, talents, and energy to those in need.

In service, we can find happiness and fulfillment on many levels. It is good for both the body and the soul. As humans, we have the instinct to care for others, but we are often distracted by the external world which makes us forget this. To live a fulfilled life (of service) we need to reconnect with that instinct.

When we serve others, it brings **us** happiness as well. Those who serve tend to live a healthier and more fulfilled life. Service is beneficial to us because it:

- **Connects us** – we meet and interact with others

- **Amplifies gratitude** – it gives us a broader view of what we have and makes us thankful

- **Increases compassion** – makes us more aware of what is needed in the world and what we can do

- **Builds self-esteem** – when you help others, it gives you a sense of purpose; you are making a difference

Selfless service does not have to be grand gestures, but can be implemented in small ways every day. For example, you may not be able to end world hunger by your charitable action of feeding one person who is hungry but as Jay says "to help any hungry person is to water the seeds of compassion". Many people in the world think only of themselves, but if you start to slowly expand your "radius of care" you would soon find yourself caring for more people.

Jay asks the question: *when will you be ready to serve?*

Many of us put off serving because we are busy trying to make our lives financially or emotionally stable first. Or we say we don't have the time **now**. But when will you have the time? Service should be an ongoing practice; you will never have enough time or money.

To adopt a service mindset, we must let go (detach) of our time and money. You don't have to have a lot of money or time to give.

Research shows that people with less tend to give more. Why is this so? Perhaps it is because those with less have been more exposed to hardship so they understand what it is like not to have. They have greater empathy for those who don't have.

To serve with intention means to serve without expecting anything in return. This is true service. If you help someone, do not expect them to help you back. If they do, good, but don't offer your service, with the expectation of it being returned. You can however take joy from serving. If being helpful makes you feel good, then that is okay. It has been said that serving can help to reduce your anxiety and stress.

Opportunities to serve are all around us if we take the time to look. You may even find that you can be of service within your own purpose (dharma). For example, there may be opportunities to serve your community using the skills or talents you already have. You can also choose where to serve, based on your compassion – what do you feel strongly about? (To explore this option, complete the exercise in the Action Checklist section below)

Key Insights from this Chapter

1. The most meaningful and fulfilling life is a life of service like the monks have.

2. We cannot all live like monks, but we can adopt a service mindset (selfless service).

3. Think about how you can serve others - within your dharma if possible.

Identify Related Issues

1. How am I serving those around me?

2. What can I do to make a difference?

3. Is there any way in which I can make use of my skills or talents to serve others?

Goals You Want to Achieve

1. To adopt a service mindset

2. To delve deeper and understand what makes life fulfilling

Your Plan of Action

1. Become more conscious of where and how I can serve.

2. Start serving – even if I start small, within my circle then move to my community, and so on.

Action Checklist

1. Make a list of 3 areas in your life where you felt pain or you felt lost or in need of help. Now match a charity or cause to one of these pains.
   For instance, as a teen, you wished there had been someone you could talk to about your depression or anxiety. So, maybe now you can volunteer in a support group for teens or join a teen hotline or a mentoring program, whichever aligns with your dharma.

   Or maybe when you were growing up you were sometimes hungry and you promised yourself that you would never be in that situation again. Extend your compassion to others in your community or the world.

Maybe you can volunteer at a soup kitchen or feeding scheme. If you don't have the time, maybe you can donate to a charity fund that feeds kids in poorer communities/schools or other countries. Remember every little bit counts.

2. If neither of the above scenarios relates to you, then do some research. A quick internet search will show you several organizations, charities, groups, etc that need volunteers or donations. Choose something that calls out to you.

Extra Exercise

Now that you have reached the end of this workbook, here is a final exercise for you to try:

Meditation through chanting – sound meditation

Throughout this workbook, we have learned how to connect to people through gratitude, relationships, and service. Sound meditation allows us to connect with our souls and the universe. We do this through words and songs by chanting or repeating mantras and affirmations during meditation.

One of the oldest and most sacred mantras is Om or as it is referred to in chanting A-U-M. The vibrations from chanting A-U-M have been shown to have some health benefits, one of which is to stimulate the vagus nerve thus decreasing inflation.

Try this:

1. Find a comfortable position—sitting in a chair, sitting upright with a cushion, or lying
down.
2. Close your eyes.
3. Lower your gaze.
4. Make yourself comfortable in this position.
5. Bring your awareness to calm, balance, ease, stillness, and peace.
6. Whenever your mind wanders, just gently and softly bring it back to calm, balance,
ease, stillness, and peace.
7. Chant each of these mantras three times each. When you chant them, bring your
attention to each syllable. Pronounce it properly so that you can hear the vibration

clearly. Really feel the mantra, repeating it genuinely and sincerely, and visualizing a
more insightful, blessed, and service-filled life.

1. OM NAMO BHAGAVATE VASUDEVAYA
"I offer praise unto the all-pervading divinity present within every heart; who is the
embodiment of beauty, intelligence, strength, wealth, fame, and detachment."
This mantra has been chanted for millennia by yogis and sages. It is cleansing and
empowering, and connects one with the divinity in everything. It can be recited especially when you are seeking insight and guidance.

2. OM TAT SAT
"The absolute truth is eternal."
This mantra appears in the Bhagavad Gita. It represents divine energy and invokes
powerful blessings. All work is performed as an offering of love and service. This mantra is recited especially before beginning any important work, to help perfect and refine our intentions and bring about balance and wholeness.

3. LOKAH SAMASTAH SUKHINO BHAVANTU

"May all beings everywhere be happy and free, and may the thoughts, words, and actions of my own life contribute in some way to that happiness and to that freedom for all."
This mantra, popularized by Jivamukti yoga, is a beautiful reminder to look beyond
ourselves and to remember our place in the universe.

Conclusion

Changing one's mindset or adopting a whole new mindset is not easy and cannot occur overnight. After reading the summaries and working your way through the exercises presented in this workbook, see if you can implement some of the strategies presented here in your life as soon as possible.

Start by training your mind gradually by becoming more aware of what you tend to focus on and what your weaknesses or strengths are. What do you feel passionate about? Discover your dharma.

Look at what you have - what can you be grateful for? How can you make improvements, if need be, in your relationships? How can you bring more gratitude and service into your life?

Perhaps you would like to start incorporating breathwork and meditation in your life on a more regular basis. Google some meditation practices and exercises, which you can include in your daily life. Or you can adopt the practices outlined in this workbook to get started in your daily routine.

If your goal is to live a purposeful, service-based, meaningful life as monks do then you will have to try your best to *think like a monk*. Adopting the monk mindset does not mean you have to live like a monk. It just requires "self-awareness, discipline, diligence, focus and constant practice" to live a purposeful and meaningful life without regrets.

May you be well and happy.

Made in the USA
Las Vegas, NV
22 December 2023

83408210R00059